THE
SCOTS AND SCOTCH-IRISH
IN AMERICA

THE SCOTS AND SCOTCH-IRISH
IN AMERICA

James E. Johnson

Lerner Publications Company · Minneapolis

Front cover: A burly contestant hurls a 56-pound weight in the Highland Games at Grandfather Mountain in western North Carolina.

Page 2: Sir Thomas J. Lipton (1850-1931), a Scot born in Glasgow, founded a huge tea-producing company. He learned the grocery business as a teenager in the United States, and, though he never became a U.S. citizen, owned many American stores, warehouses, and stockyards. Later in life he challenged U.S. yacht racers five times—unsuccessfully—for the America's Cup trophy.

1991 REVISED EDITION

Johnson, James E.
    The Scots and Scotch-Irish in America / James E. Johnson. Minneapolis, Lerner Publications Co. © 1991

    72 p. ill., ports. 24 cm. (The In America Series)

    A brief history of the Scots and Scotch-Irish, their immigration and settlement in the United States, and their contributions to American life and culture.

    1. Scots–United States 2. Scots-Irish–United States I. Title # Series.

E184.S3J6   1991   973'.049163
ISBN 0-8225-0242-9 (lib. bdg.)
ISBN 0-8225-1038-3 (pbk.)

Manufactured in the United States of America

1 2 3 4 5 6 7 8 9 10 00 99 98 97 96 95 94 93 92 91

CONTENTS

1
FROM SEPARATE ISLES

With well-timed leaps and kicks, girls perform a vigorous Scottish reel at a Highland Games festival in northern Virginia.

Scots and Scotch-Irish

The difference between the Scots and the Scotch-Irish is historical, not ethnic. Both the Scots and the Scotch-Irish trace their origins ultimately to Scotland—the northern part of the United Kingdom's largest island. An American family of Scotch-Irish descent, however, has ancestors who once lived in Northern Ireland before immigrating to the United States. This connection with Northern Ireland (also called Ulster) is the basis for distinguishing between the Scots (who came directly from Scotland) and the Scotch-Irish.

The Scotch-Irish are not part Scots and part Irish. Intermarriage in Ulster between the Catholic Irish and the Protestant Scots was rare. The Scotch-Irish are ethnically Scots.

Still, they deserve a separate designation. To the Scots of Ulster, Ireland was home. Their living conditions were different from those of the Scots just across the North Channel. They came to the United States for different reasons and settled in different places than did the Scots from Scotland.

For many reasons, these immigrants from Ulster could more easily have called themselves Irish than Scots. They sometimes did—until the United States attracted hundreds of thousands of Catholic Irish immigrants in the middle of the 19th century. At that point, determined to distinguish themselves as Protestants (and therefore to avoid anti-Catholic prejudice in the United States), Ulster Scots grew more content with the term *Scotch-Irish*.

The Scots themselves dislike being called Scotch. Properly known as Scots—or, perhaps, as the Scottish—they are not shy about informing others that scotch is a kind of whiskey, not a kind of person.

Keeping track of the number of Scots and Scotch-Irish immigrants to the United States is difficult. Neither Scotland nor Northern Ireland has been a nation at any time during U.S. history. In 1707, long before the United States was founded, Scotland was fully united with England to form the Kingdom of Great Britain. Even before Northern Ireland was officially absorbed into the United Kingdom in 1801, it was considered merely a part of Ireland. Consequently, people coming from Scotland to the United States would be counted as being from Great Britain. People coming from Northern Ireland would be immigrants either from Ireland or from the United Kingdom.

In an official sense, there was no separate country of origin for such immigrants. The U.S. Immigration and Naturalization Service does not count the number of Scots or Scotch-Irish entering the United States. All such people are officially immigrants from the United Kingdom.

Most people of Scots or Scotch-Irish background, however, consider themselves different from the English or the Welsh or the other peoples of the United Kingdom. These Scots and Scotch-Irish proudly point out exactly what their ethnic background is. In the 1980 U.S. census, 10,048,816 persons—slightly more than 5 percent of all the people listing any specific ethnic background—reported being of at least partial Scottish ancestry.

Highlands, Lowlands, and Ulster

Scotland is hilly near its border with England and mountainous in the northwest. Between these two areas lies a flatter region that is the center of agriculture and industry in the country. These Lowlands are also home to a vast majority (nearly three-quarters) of Scotland's people. Both of Scotland's largest cities, Glasgow and Edinburgh, are in the Lowlands.

The Highlands in the northwest cover more territory than do the Lowlands, but they are far less heavily populated. The Highlands are also historically distinct from the Lowlands. The Gaelic language and other Celtic traditions have found a stronghold in

The British Isles

NORTH ATLANTIC OCEAN

NORTH SEA

SCOTLAND

HIGHLANDS

CENTRAL LOWLANDS

Edinburgh

ULSTER (NORTHERN IRELAND)

Glasgow

SOUTHERN UPLANDS

North Channel

Londonderry

Belfast

EIRE (REPUBLIC OF IRELAND)

IRISH SEA

Dublin

WALES

ENGLAND

London

The United Kingdom of Great Britain and Northern Ireland encompasses England, Scotland, Wales, the northeastern part of Ireland, and several small nearby islands.

the Highlands. Clans (large family groupings that were almost like self-governing tribes) remained central to Highland society long after they had lost influence in the Lowlands. Most of Scotland had become Protestant by the end of the 16th century, but the Highlands continued to have many pockets of Roman Catholicism.

The northeastern tip of Northern Ireland lies less than 20 miles (32 kilometers) from the coast of Scotland. That closeness, however, does not fully explain the large number of Scots-descended people in Ulster.

Among the many rebellions against English rule in Ireland, the one most significant for Ulster was the revolt by two northern leaders, the earls of Tyrconnel and Tyrone, in the early 1600s. Once English forces had finally defeated these Irish leaders in 1607, the English government encouraged Protestants from England and Scotland to settle in certain Irish counties. These new settlers would theoretically be more loyal to the Protestant monarchs of England than the Catholic Irish had been. The Irish were forced to move aside and make room for the Protestant newcomers.

This scheme to alter the population of Ireland (known as the Plantation of Ireland) brought tens of thousands of Lowland Scots to Ulster—especially to the counties of Tyrone, Donegal, Londonderry, and Antrim—in the early 1600s. Later, as Protestant rule in Northern Ireland became more secure, even more Scots went. English supporters of the Plantation scheme had hoped that the new settlers in Ulster would be mostly English. Scottish Lowlanders, however, far outnumbered the English. By the end of the 17th century, the number of Scots who had moved to Northern Ireland had almost certainly surpassed 100,000. The number of English settlers was probably not even half that.

These Scots went to Ulster partially, but not entirely, for economic reasons. Workers in the mills or factories might escape unemployment by moving to Ireland. Some farmers saw opportunity in Ireland. Still, most of the farmers settling in Ulster would merely be working land that they rented from English landowners. Rents might be lower than they were in Scotland, but these settlers got no free land.

For many of the Lowland Scots, a move to Ireland was primarily a move away from religious strife in Scotland. Religious conflict in Britain was not limited to fighting between Protestants and Catholics. Among the Protestants, disputes over religious and administrative issues often led to violence. No issue was more divisive among Scottish Protestants than the argument between the Presbyterians and the Episcopalians.

The Presbyterians, strongly influenced by the teachings of reformers like John Calvin and John Knox, believed that the elders—or presbyters—of a congregation should administer

John Knox

the affairs of the church. In such a church organization, the leaders at various levels are elected by the group they lead. This conflicted with the way the Church of Scotland was organized. Especially before the 1690s, the Church of Scotland—the Scottish counterpart of the Church of England—was administered by bishops. These bishops were appointed by central authorities in the church and, in turn, exercised control over several congregations within a region. This was called an episcopal system, from the Latin word *episcopus*, meaning "bishop."

The debate over whether the Church of Scotland should have a Presbyterian or Episcopalian organization involved countless other issues as well. Each side in the Presbyterian-Episcopalian debate advocated its own positions in matters of doctrine, morality, and personal behavior. For a short time during the mid-1600s, the Presbyterians appeared to have won the debate. After 1660, however, the episcopal system was brought back to the Church of Scotland and the Presbyterians, even though they were very numerous, found themselves at odds with the established church in Scotland. Even after 1690, when the Church of Scotland ceased to enjoy special legal privileges that other religions were denied, the debate between Presbyterians and Episcopalians continued.

The most heavily Presbyterian area of Scotland was in the Lowlands. These Lowlanders saw the Church of Scotland rejecting their reforms—and began to experience persecution for their beliefs. Many concluded that they could worship more freely if they moved to Ulster, away from the Episcopalians with whom they had been arguing for so long.

In Ireland, they would have to live among Catholics, but the gulf between Irish Catholics and Scottish Protestants was very wide. The two groups might be able simply to ignore each other's religions. The Scots were living in Ireland, but they were not Irish. Intermarriage with the local Catholics was out of the question. Also, the Scotch-Irish were living on land that had been taken away from the Irish, who resented the intrusion. Trust between the two groups would have been hard to establish. The Presbyterian Scots hoped to establish Protestant enclaves in Northern Ireland that were solidly Presbyterian.

Presbyterianism did thrive among these Scots in Ulster. Still, any hopes they had of practicing their religion in isolation—either from the Catholics or from episcopal-minded Protestants— were to be dashed. After the Catholic king of England, James II, was driven from the throne in 1688, his supporters in Ireland refused to obey the Protestants who had displaced him. A bitter civil war ensued, and the Scotch-Irish, who supported the new Protestant king, William of Orange, found themselves at war with the Catholics who supported James II. Battles between Protestants and Catholics at Enniskillen and at Londonderry were fierce. This war ended in 1690 after King William's forces won the famous Battle of the Boyne in Ireland, but more conflict lay ahead for the Scotch-Irish who were Presbyterians.

In order to make sure that civic leaders supported official church policy, the English Parliament passed a law, the Test Act, in 1704. The Test Act said that only people who took communion in the Church of England (often called the Anglican church) could hold important civic or military positions in British territories. The Presbyterians, like many other groups of Protestants, disagreed with the Church of England about the meaning of the communion ritual. They considered it wrong to take communion with the Anglicans. This meant that the Presbyterian Scotch-Irish could not hold political offices in Ulster—or even become officers in the military.

For the Presbyterians among the Scotch-Irish, Ulster was turning out to be a poor refuge from religious controversy. Many began to look elsewhere.

The Move to America

North America effectively opened up to the Scots and Scotch-Irish as it opened up to the English. Unlike other immigrant groups, the Scots and the Scotch-Irish—because they spoke English and because most of them were literate—were able to arrange many details of their immigration before they left their homeland. Moving to a new country is rarely easy, but the Scots and Scotch-Irish were less likely than other immigrants to be tricked into bad business deals by unscrupulous North Americans. They also were able to blend easily into the population of the British colonies. Their accents might set them apart from other British settlers, but any prejudice they might encounter because of their speech was minor.

The Scots

The Scots often immigrated to America in groups. Many members of a Highland clan, for example, might leave Scotland together. Associations of Lowlanders might be formed to pool their money and buy land in America.

One distinct group of Scottish immigrants settled in America just before the outbreak of the American Revolution. About 12,000 Highlanders fought in the British army during the conflict that is usually called the French and Indian War (1754-1763). Only 76 of these soldiers returned to the Highlands when the war was over. The others were probably induced to stay in America by the British government's offer of a good deal on American land to those who had served in the army. (Good farmland was hard to find in

Highland cattle with thick fur graze on a hillside in Argyllshire in western Scotland. The Highlands provide enough grass to support herds of cattle and sheep, but the chilly climate and stony soil limit the planting of crops. Many of the Highland Scots who left for America were searching for better farmland.

the cold and stony Highlands of Scotland.) Most of these former soldiers settled in New York and on Prince Edward Island in Canada.

In November 1767, another group of Scots landed in southeastern North Carolina. The governor of the colony, William Tryon, granted them free land in Cumberland and Mecklenburg counties at the rate of 100 acres per person. One family with four children even somehow got 640 acres—40 beyond their allotment. Good parcels of that size were almost unimaginable to the Scots Highlanders, who were more familiar with farms of some 10 or 12 acres.

Especially during the 1600s, some of the Scots who came to North America had no choice in the matter. Convicts from Great Britain—usually petty criminals, debtors, and people imprisoned for their political or religious beliefs—were routinely shipped to North America because there was not enough room for them in British prisons.

Mostly, however, the Highlanders and Lowlanders who left Scotland did so voluntarily, and usually for economic reasons. Crop failures, low cattle prices, unemployment, and evictions from their farms convinced many Scots that life in another land would hold more promise. Social changes, such as the decreasing influence of clan leaders in the Highlands, displaced many people and set them in search of something new.

Stories had come back to Scotland that North America had no titled landlords to tyrannize the farmer. Scottish farmers who were merely tenants working someone else's land looked forward to owning their own farms. They came to look upon America as a place of cheap land, low taxes, high wages, and a healthy climate.

The reality of America did not quite match that ideal. Many emigrants could not immediately fulfill their dreams of independent land ownership. The cost of a trans-Atlantic move was very high. Many could obtain passage only as indentured servants — workers who were given transportation to America but who were obligated to spend several years working for the person who had paid for their tickets. Only after they had worked off the cost of their passage were they free to choose another way of life. Still, many Scots were willing to put up with the inconvenience. One gentleman in Glasgow, writing in 1774 to a friend in Philadelphia, said, "The distress of the common people here is deeper and more general than you can imagine. There is an almost total stagnation in our manufactures, and grain is dear; many hundreds of labourers and mechanics, especially weavers in this neighborhood, have lately indented and gone to America."

The rumor that there were no landlords in America also proved false. Just before the American Revolution, one major landowner in New York State, Sir William Johnson, convinced a large number of Highlanders to settle on his lands in the Mohawk Valley. Johnson built up a sort of private kingdom there. He was a good landlord, but he compelled his tenants to have their grain ground at his mill. This obligation between tenants and landlord was very similar to practices the Highlanders had just left behind in Scotland.

As unrest in the North American colonies increased, the British government became alarmed at the growing number of Scots leaving for America. These emigrants might pick up radical American principles, the British feared, and become at once a loss to the British army and a gain to the American. Consequently, emigration from Scotland for America was prohibited in 1775.

While Scottish newspapers contained advertisements from America

A weaver in County Donegal (once part of Northern Ireland but now in the Republic of Ireland) works at his loom. Textiles have long been a specialty of Ulster, and numerous skilled weavers emigrated for America after the British Parliament restricted the export of Irish textiles.

calling for carpenters, blacksmiths, masons, and other artisans, the British government occasionally worried that too many skilled workers were leaving. Especially after the United States had won its independence from Great Britain, the British government occasionally tried to stop the emigration of skilled Scottish workers in such industries as textile weaving.

The Scotch-Irish

During the 1700s, a steady stream of Scotch-Irish emigrants poured out of Ulster to other parts of the world. The most important reasons for this migration were economic pressures and religious persecution.

To protect British manufacturers of woolen products, through most of the 17th century, the British government prohibited the importation of Irish woolen goods into Scotland, England, and British holdings in America. But the British woolen industry still protested. As a result, the English Parliament in 1699 went further and prohibited the Irish from exporting manufactured wool "to any other country whatever." To the Scotch-Irish, many of whom were in the textile business, this was a severe blow.

In 1717 and 1718, many Scotch-Irish farmers were evicted when they refused, or were unable, to pay higher rents to their English landlords. Many of these uprooted farmers had been

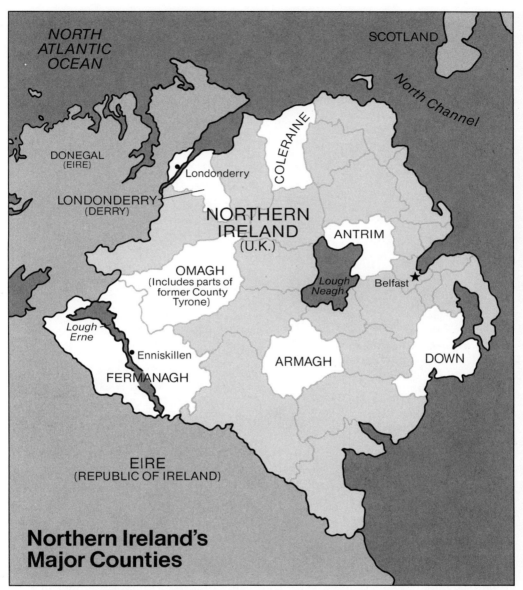

NORTH
ATLANTIC
OCEAN

SCOTLAND

North Channel

DONEGAL
(EIRE)

Londonderry

COLERAINE

LONDONDERRY
(DERRY)

NORTHERN
IRELAND
(U.K.)

ANTRIM

OMAGH
(Includes parts of
former County
Tyrone)

Lough
Neagh

Belfast

Lough
Erne

Enniskillen

ARMAGH

DOWN

FERMANAGH

EIRE
(REPUBLIC OF IRELAND)

Northern Ireland's Major Counties

Certain areas of Northern Ireland—such as Londonderry, Armagh, Fermanagh, and Tyrone—attracted especially large numbers of Protestants from Scotland. (Most of what used to be County Tyrone is now called County Omagh.) County Donegal, though now part of the Republic of Ireland (Eire), was once part of the province of Ulster and also drew numerous Scottish settlers.

British troops attempt to evict Irish tenants. High rents drove many Ulster Scots out of their Irish homes and toward new lives in America.

than 12,000 left annually. In the half century before the American Revolution, perhaps 200,000 persons, or one-third of the Protestant population of Ulster, emigrated, the majority going to America. Some authorities in Ireland feared that the country would lose most of its skilled inhabitants. Archbishop Boulter, Lord Primate of All Ireland, writing in 1728, said: "The whole north is in a ferment at present, and people every day encouraging one another to go. . . . The worst is, that it affects only Protestants, and reigns chiefly in the north, which is the seat of our linen manufacture."

Although most Scotch-Irish immigrants to America probably left for economic reasons, religious difficulties also played a part in the large-scale emigrations of the 1700s. Even before the Test Act was passed in 1704, restrictions on Presbyterian preachers were periodically put into place. The Test Act, however, was much more than a mere annoyance. It effectively made second-class citizens out of the Presbyterians and other non-Anglicans. Some very capable leaders were prevented from holding public office. Although the Test Act was repealed in 1782, many Scotch-Irish lost patience long before that.

The emigrants who left Ulster were subjected to the usual dangers of an ocean crossing. The ships were often unsafe for such a journey and usually very overcrowded. Seldom was enough water taken for the entire voyage, and

just barely surviving anyway. After a few bad harvests, many of them would probably have been unable to pay even a reasonable rent. Crops throughout Ulster did poorly in the late 1720s, and outright famine struck in 1741. As English landlords kept pressing the increasingly desperate people of Ulster for higher rents, some Scotch-Irish tenants struck back by damaging their landlords' property. Others decided that it was time to leave.

More than 4,000 left for America in 1718. After the famine of 1741, more

16

what there was often stank. Most people added vinegar to the water to weaken its stench before drinking it. The food often became moldy and rotten.

Dysentery was a constant danger. The dreaded "ship's fever" usually meant an outbreak of cholera and almost daily burials at sea. Storms at sea made life particularly miserable for the passengers since they were then confined below deck for long periods of time. Many of them had only straw for beds, and when this became damp and moldy it had to be thrown overboard.

One especially terrible story was that of the *Seaflower*, which sailed for Philadelphia from the Ulster port of Belfast on July 10, 1741, with 106 persons aboard. They had barely begun the voyage when the captain died and the first mate was taken ill. The mast split, the crew could not navigate properly, and provisions ran low. In order to stay alive, the living began to eat the dead. After six bodies had been eaten, the *Success*, a man-of-war, came along and supplied the remaining passengers with food for the rest of the trip. By the time the voyage ended late in October, 46 people had died.

Crop failures in the early 1700s made bad times even worse for many farmers in Northern Ireland. In this illustration, children help their mother search for a few edible potatoes in a blighted field.

2
AN AMERICAN WAY OF LIFE

A Scotch-Irish farmhouse at the Frontier Culture Museum of Virginia replicates the type of lodging common among Scotch-Irish immigrants to the United States in the 18th and 19th centuries.

The Scots Settle In

Most of the Scots who came to America could quickly find a place in colonial society. Language problems did not force the Scots into little communities where a few old-timers had to translate for confused newcomers. Although many immigrants from the Highlands spoke Gaelic, they generally could also speak English. They sometimes drew together out of an interest in speaking Gaelic, but not out of necessity.

If a prospective Scots emigrant had been receiving letters from someone who had already moved to America, any American location recommended in those letters would probably receive first consideration. America was a big, diverse place, and it was only natural for a newcomer to take the advice of an experienced resident. The comfort of knowing someone in an American town would often influence Scots immigrants to choose a place where acquaintances had already settled.

Many Scots decided on an American destination long before they even set out across the sea. By accepting indentured service with a given employer, a Scottish immigrant also accepted an American destination—at least for the first few years. In other cases, when an immigrant was traveling to America as part of a group, the arrangements made in Scotland often specified exactly where the group would settle. The group might have already purchased land as part of the emigration plan.

Some of the American colonies, especially in the south, offered land at very good prices—sometimes even for free—to Scots immigrants. Such offers drew many Scots to North Carolina, for example. The colony of Georgia was heavily promoted by colonial officials and by shipowners who were eager to sell trans-Atlantic tickets to passengers.

A Scot's occupation greatly affected the choice of an American destination. Many of the immigrants in the 1700s were farmers, and they wanted farmland. Such settlers were more likely to choose rural locations in Pennsylvania or North Carolina or Georgia than to settle in Boston or Philadelphia. Scottish textile workers were likely to head for the mill towns of New England. Especially later, in the 19th century, many immigrants had very specialized skills in one industry or another. If they chose to settle in an American town where their skills could not be applied, they were likely to remain just as unemployed as they had been in Scotland.

Overall, the settlement of Scottish immigrants in America mirrors the east-to-west expansion of the British colonies. The coastal area attracted the earliest Scots settlers. Later, frontier areas near the foothills of the Appalachians and new settlements along interior rivers and lakes drew their share of the Scots. As America moved westward, so did the Scots.

The Scotch-Irish Niche

Scotch-Irish immigrants to America followed a different pattern of settlement. Although the coastal region of America certainly attracted many of them, the Scotch-Irish often headed directly for the frontier—partly because they wanted to go there and partly because they received a cold reception elsewhere.

New England

The Puritans of New England and the Scotch-Irish Presbyterians seemed to have a lot in common. Both groups held Calvinist beliefs. They both opposed the established Church of England and felt oppressed by its policies. For this reason some of the early Scotch-Irish emigrants headed for New England.

A worker at a restored Scotch-Irish farm feeds one of her hens. The cart in the background was used for carrying peat and sod.

From 1714 through 1720, about 54 vessels arrived in Boston from Ireland, most of them from Ulster. The New England authorities were eager to settle the Scotch-Irish on the frontier, where they could absorb most of the hostility between European colonists and the Native Americans. The Surveyor-General of Customs at Boston, Thomas Lechmere, wrote in 1718 that the Scotch-Irish "are come over hither for no other reason but upon encouragement sent from hence... that they should have so many acres of land given them gratis to settle our frontiers as a barrier against the Indians."

Other than accepting the value of the Scotch-Irish as border guards, however, New Englanders generally did not welcome them. The two groups found many differences between their types of Protestantism. Each side accused the other of tolerating incorrect religious practices. In addition, the Scotch-Irish were simply not English, and to many New Englanders that was bad enough.

Cotton Mather, one of the most famous ministers in the Massachusetts Bay Colony, opposed the plans for allowing Scotch-Irish settlements— even on the frontier—as "formidable attempts of Satan and his Sons to

Unsettle us." Scotch-Irish property at Worcester, Massachusetts, was destroyed by a mob one night. Eventually, most of the Scotch-Irish at Worcester moved to Pelham, farther west. The Scotch-Irish arrivals in Boston were usually hurried out of the city as fast as possible. The excuses given were many, but as one official wrote in 1718, "these confounded Irish will eat us all up, provisions being most extravagantly dear and scarce of all sorts."

One group of settlers who arrived in Boston in August 1718 chose a place on the frontier that had been called Nutfield (because of an abundance of chestnut, walnut, and butternut trees). The settlers renamed the place Londonderry in honor of a city in Ulster. By 1734, according to church records, 700 people received communion there. Londonderry, New Hampshire, became a thriving community where flax and potatoes were cultivated and where many residents manufactured linen in their homes. The McClellands, Campbells, McDonalds, McGregors, McNeils, Magills, and Fergusons were among the prominent families of this American Londonderry.

By building with rough logs, Scotch-Irish settlers on the American frontier could quickly construct a church—one of the most essential structures in a frontier Presbyterian community.

The mixed reception given to the Scotch-Irish in New England turned the stream of Ulster settlers further south. Although there were over 500 Scotch-Irish settlements in America at the time of the Revolution, only 70 were in New England.

These immigrants did leave their mark on New England. The Scotch-Irish taught their Puritan neighbors how to cultivate and cook with potatoes. They also laid the foundation for a spinning and weaving industry. Other colonies, however, offered attractive opportunities, and the Scotch-Irish were not slow to take advantage of them.

Pennsylvania

Reports that filtered back to Ulster from Scotch-Irish immigrants in Pennsylvania were encouraging.

After breaking through the village's stockade, Native Americans attack a Scotch-Irish settlement on the frontier. Because the Scotch-Irish were encouraged to settle on the very edges of the wilderness, fighting between them and the Native Americans was frequent. Colonial governors in New England and in Pennsylvania deliberately used these Ulster Scots as buffers between the Native Americans and colonial cities.

These settlers praised the colony's liberal laws, low taxes, and freedom—economic, social, and religious. The only other colony to offer such liberty was Rhode Island, and Rhode Island had its drawbacks. It was a limited area, it had been settled before, and the land in Rhode Island was not as fertile as that of Pennsylvania. All in all, Pennsylvania appeared to be the home that the Scotch-Irish had been seeking as an alterative to inhospitable New England.

The Scotch-Irish began to arrive in Pennsylvania in great numbers and caused James Logan, the provincial secretary of Pennsylvania, to write in 1727 that "we have from the North of Ireland great numbers...eight or nine ships...discharged at Newcastle." He later added, "It looks as if Ireland is to send all its inhabitants hither, for last week not less than six ships arrived, and every day, two or three arrive also." By 1749, the Scotch-Irish composed about one-fourth of the whole population of Pennsylvania.

The early settlers in Pennsylvania moved up the river valleys, particularly those of the Susquehanna and Delaware. The stream of Scotch-Irish settlers flowed around the Quaker settlements and into the back country, where they set up their cabins, their mills, and their Presbyterian churches. The Susquehanna and Cumberland valleys became strongholds of Scotch-Irish influence. Such towns as Chambersburg, Gettysburg, Carlisle, and York are still home to many descendants of these early Scotch-Irish settlers.

The government of Pennsylvania had mixed feelings about these Ulster Scots. Here too, as in New England, the Scotch-Irish on the frontier formed a barrier that insulated other Europeans from hostile Native Americans. In 1729, Secretary Logan of Pennsylvania wrote a letter in which he explained his plans regarding the Scotch-Irish settlers:

> About this time [1720] a considerable number of people came in from Ireland who wanted to be settled, at the same time it happened that we were under the same apprehensions from northern Indians.... I therefore thought it might be prudent to plant a settlement of fresh men as those who formerly had so bravely defended Enniskillen and Derry as a frontier in case of any disturbance.

Despite their value as a buffer on the frontier, the Scotch-Irish were a worry to the government of Pennsylvania. Some of them, perhaps remembering their unhappy experiences with skyrocketing rents in Ulster, simply refused to pay any rent for the land they occupied. Many of the Scotch-Irish settlers in Pennsylvania occupied the land as squatters—they settled wherever they pleased without asking anyone's permission. Secretary Logan wrote in 1730 that the Scotch-Irish had settled on Conestoga Manor, a tract of 15,000 acres that the Penn family—the English founders of Pennsylvania—had reserved for themselves. Logan stated that he did not know how to get these people off the land since the Scotch-Irish claimed that it was "against the laws of God and nature that so much land should be idle when so many Christians wanted it to labor on." Other Scotch-Irish settlers were later accused of harassing, even of massacring, groups of Native Americans. Secretary Logan wrote in 1730 that the "settlement of five families from Ireland gives me more trouble than fifty of any other people."

The Scotch-Irish usually landed at Philadelphia and proceeded to the interior to find a place to settle. By 1730, Pennsylvania had its Derry, Donegal, Tyrone, and Coleraine townships. There was a Toboyne in Derry County, and a Fermanagh Township in Juniata County, as well as an Ulster and a Chester County. The Donegal, Paxtany, Derry, and Hanover townships, some lands north of Wilmington, and the Allen township west of Easton were the earliest Scotch-Irish settlements in Pennsylvania.

The Scotch-Irish settlements in Lancaster, Lebanon, Dauphin, and York counties were in a region that was attracting many German settlers. The Scotch-Irish soon found themselves surrounded by unfamiliar neighbors with whom they did not get along especially well. The differences between the two groups ran the gamut from religion to farming methods. The Scotch-Irish, for example, did not share the German passion for meticulous organization on the farm. A Scotch-Irish farmer, after cutting down the trees that grew on a parcel of farmland, would simply plant between the stumps. A German farmer would pull the stumps out, vastly improving the efficiency of the farm. In the 1740s, in order to reduce the friction between the Scotch-Irish and the Germans, the Pennsylvania authorities stopped selling land in this area to the Scotch-Irish and offered them a good price on land farther west. Many of the Scotch-Irish settlers accepted this offer and sold out to the Germans.

East of the Susquehanna River, the Scotch-Irish were outnumbered by both the English and the Germans. West of the Susquehanna, as far as the Allegheny Mountains, they were the most numerous national group. Western Pennsylvania became a distinct section, occupied predominantly by Scotch-Irish. Their predominance in this region had an important effect on politics in Pennsylvania.

The Scotch-Irish became involved in Pennsylvania politics at a very early date, forming a political party that opposed the established leaders. From the beginning they came into conflict with the Quaker government. The most serious clash took place over the question of military preparedness and was brought to a head by the French and Indian War (1754-1763).

The Quakers, a religious group famous for its absolute opposition to all kinds of war, had governed the colony of Pennsylvania since it was founded in 1682. The Scotch-Irish had no moral problem with fighting to protect themselves and their property. In 1755, General Edward Braddock, who commanded the British troops in western Pennsylvania, was defeated by a combined French and Native American force. This left the residents of western Pennsylvania wide open to attack.

The residents of this area, most of whom were Scotch-Irish, appealed to the Quaker-dominated government for help in fighting the French and the Native Americans. The Quakers refused. The Scotch-Irish were incensed not only by this refusal but by what they saw as an unjust political monopoly enjoyed by the Quakers in Pennsylvania's government. (In 1755, the Quakers, who constituted only one-fifth of Pennsylvania's population, held 26 of the 36 seats in the Pennsylvania Assembly.) Some of the Quakers in the assembly resigned their seats so that persons without moral prohibitions against war could step in, but the people of the frontier were not satisfied.

The Scotch-Irish took matters into their own hands. They erected forts and raised a volunteer army to defend them. They also encouraged these vigilantes to be merciless with any Native Americans seen near European towns.

A Scotch-Irish farmer surveys his stump-cluttered field. Like other Scotch-Irish farmers in America, he has simply planted his crops between the stumps.

Some volunteer soldiers in eastern Pennsylvania attacked a completely peaceful group of Native Americans near Bethlehem and Lancaster and massacred them even though the Native Americans offered no resistance.

The frontier settlers continued to denounce the Pennsylvania Assembly in Philadelphia for inaction. Finally a group of residents from the townships of Lebanon, Paxton, and Hanover decided to march on Philadelphia. This group, known as the Paxton Boys, threatened to sack Philadelphia and

For SALE, or BARTER,
A Quantity of L A N D in Patents,
from 250 to 1000 Acres, situate in Botetourt and Mononga-
hela Counties, Virginia, will be sold very low for Cash, Pro-
duce, any Kind of Certificates, or Indents, good Bonds, Land,
or other Property in the State of Maryland. For Terms, ap-
ply to

J. Williams.

Annapolis, May 12, 1789.

to kill a group of Christian Native Americans who were being sheltered there. These Native Americans had been converted, by German settlers, to a Christian denomination known as Moravianism. With frontier vigilantes on the march against all Native Americans, General Thomas Gage and a company of British soldiers had to be brought to Philadelphia to guard them. In the end, the conflict was resolved at a conference just outside the city of Philadelphia, but only because the city was able to call upon such able negotiators as Benjamin Franklin to calm the Paxton Boys down.

Maryland, Virginia, the Carolinas, and New York

Many of the Scotch-Irish settlers in Maryland, Virginia, and the Carolinas had settled first in Pennsylvania and then moved southward. They had left Pennsylvania for a variety of reasons. For one thing, the colony's government failed to protect frontier settlements. For another, the Allegheny Mountains impeded further westward expansion. It was simpler to follow the valleys going south than to penetrate the mountains to the west. Also, the land further south was cheap—only about one-third what farmland cost in Pennsylvania.

This movement south was in its early stages when Robert Harper, a Scotch-Irish pioneer, settled at the junction of the Shenandoah and Potomac rivers in 1735 and founded Harper's Ferry, Virginia. As they moved down the Shenandoah Valley, the Scotch-Irish founded the Virginia towns of Staunton, Lexington, and Fincastle. There are few places in America where the Scotch-Irish influence is more clearly seen than in Augusta and Rockbridge counties in Virginia. The Scotch-Irish are credited with the founding of Washington and Lee University in that area and with establishing the region as one of the strongholds of Presbyterianism.

Many Scotch-Irish settlers reached the Carolinas by traveling down the Shenandoah Valley of Virginia and, after a short stay there, moving further south. They settled in large numbers in such North Carolina counties as Granville, Orange, Rowan, Mecklenburg, Guilford, and Davidson. The Scotch-Irish established many schools and churches in North Carolina. They spread the Presbyterian religion throughout the area and were mainly responsible for establishing Davidson College. Some Scotch-Irish settlers pushed even further south, into the piedmont country of South Carolina.

Kentucky, too, was influenced by Pennsylvania Scotch-Irish settlers who moved down the Shenandoah Valley of Virginia. From there they

Ashe County and its neighboring counties in northwestern North Carolina drew large numbers of Scots and Scotch-Irish immigrants.

proceeded to western North Carolina and then on the Wilderness Road across the mountains into Kentucky. Others moved into western Pennsylvania and then on into Ohio.

It was not until the great wave of Ulster emigration in 1718 that New York and New Jersey felt the impact of the Scotch-Irish. In 1720, settlers in the vicinity of Goshen, in New York's Orange County, were numerous enough to form a Presbyterian congregation. In the next decade, some 40 families from the north of Ireland settled in the country west of the Hudson in what became Orange and Ulster counties.

The Presbyterian Church

One of the permanent Scotch-Irish contributions to American culture is the Presbyterian church. By 1776, each of the approximately 500 Scotch-Irish communities in America, from New England to Georgia, had at least one Presbyterian congregation.

The Scotch-Irish Presbyterian preachers were usually close behind the first settlers; many even led their congregations through the wilderness to found new settlements. These ministers knew how to use a rifle and a plow and were as much at home felling a tree with an axe as preaching from the pulpit. Many of these ministers were powerful orators or scholars.

As soon as a church had been founded, the next thought of a Presbyterian preacher was to get a school started, and eventually perhaps a college. They were stern in their insistence that young people learn the catechism.

Many preachers would ride far afield to reach a frontier Presbyterian congregation that had no minister of its own. Such traveling ministers, known as circuit riders, might not return to home base for weeks or months. Their journeys required great physical stamina, but the dedication and toughness of these circuit riders—along with their learning—made them a powerful force in the Scotch-Irish frontier communities. On numerous occasions, the civil authorities appealed to Presbyterian ministers to help them maintain law and order. Some of the rougher characters on the frontier would ignore a constable but fall into line after a stern word from a preacher.

The first Presbyterian church in Pennsylvania, and perhaps in the nation, had its origin in the missionary labors of Francis Makemie, a Scotch-Irish minister from County Donegal, Ireland. Makemie visited Philadelphia in 1692 and gathered a congregation of Presbyterians who, in 1698, formed the First Presbyterian Church of Philadelphia under Reverend Jedekiah Andrews. In population and position, Philadelphia was then more like a national capital than any other town in the colonies. Almost all of the great early organizers of Presbyterianism in

America were connected in some way with the Philadelphia Presbytery.

One interesting indication of the Scotch-Irish influence on the Presbyterian church is in the names given to the presbyteries—or church districts—in the United States. The first New England presbytery was organized in about 1729 and named Londonderry. Donegal Presbytery and Carlisle Presbytery, both in Pennsylvania, were founded in 1732 and 1765, respectively.

The Scotch-Irish Presbyterians took their religion very seriously. The splits between Presbyterians, although they seemed trivial to outsiders, were often very serious to the individuals involved. One observer in western Pennsylvania reported that a married couple of that district had lived together for more than 50 years but that the man had never attended his wife's church, nor had she attended his. They were both Presbyterians, but when they reached a certain fork in the road each Sabbath day, she took their daughters to her church, and he took their sons to his.

The Scotch-Irish in Ulster had easily obtained an educated clergy because it was not difficult for a prospective minister to go to Scotland for training. Educated ministers, therefore, accompanied the Scotch-Irish immigrants from Ulster. If American-born Presbyterians, however, were to become well-educated ministers, institutions of learning would have to be set up.

A Presbyterian circuit rider

Many Presbyterian pastors founded classical schools, known as academies, so that young people in their congregations could prepare for a higher education. In 1716 William Tennent, an Ulster minister and graduate of Edinburgh, moved to America. He applied to the Synod of Philadelphia and accepted a position at a church in Neshaming, Pennsylvania. The government of the colony gave Tennent 50 acres of land on Neshaming Creek, and Tennent put up a schoolhouse on the site. This school became the influential Log College.

3
FORMING A NEW NATION

Patrick Henry, eloquent Patriot orator and the first governor of the Commonwealth of Virginia

Tories and Patriots

Once the American Revolution had begun, residents of the colonies had hard choices to make. Many attempted to stay neutral, but it was hard to avoid supporting either the rebels or the British crown. The Scots and Scotch-Irish, like the general population of the American colonies, were divided on this issue.

Many Scots were loyalists (often called Tories)—people who remained loyal to the British government and who opposed independence for America. Their ties to Scotland, which had been totally united with England for more than half a century, were strong. Most of these people had moved to America for economic reasons, not because of any dispute with the British. Many—born in Great Britain and living in a British colony—still considered themselves British and were not eager to be anything else.

Scots Tories (especially Highlanders) were numerous in the Mohawk Valley of New York, in North Carolina, and throughout the colonies. Groups of Scots in America even formed regiments to fight on the British side during the Revolution, and the Battle of King's Mountain in North Carolina pitted Scots Tories against Scotch-Irish rebels. As prospects grew dim for a British victory in the Revolution, Scots loyalists began moving north to Canada, which was still under British control. The pro-British conservatism of the great majority of Scots in the colonies exposed them to increasing abuse from Americans. Those Scots loyalists who decided to stay in the newly independent United States had to change their conception of what it meant to be an American.

Despite the widespread sympathy for the British among Scottish Americans, the rebels (often called Patriots) could claim many Scots supporters as well. For example, two signers of the Declaration of Independence were Scots immigrants—James Wilson, who had come from Carskerdo, Scotland, and John Witherspoon from Gifford, Scotland. After the British closed the port of Boston in retaliation for the Boston Tea Party, delegates at a meeting in Carlisle, Pennsylvania, condemned the British action. They chose deputies to be sent to a provincial convention, and James Wilson was among them.

Although Scots emigrants from Ulster were more likely to declare allegiance to the Patriot cause, some Scotch-Irish were Tories. Especially in the larger cities, Ulster Scots who had no particular resentment against the British supported—and even fought for—the loyalist cause. Some Scotch-Irish settlers disliked upper-class Patriots more than they disliked the British and were not willing to join forces with the rebels.

Nevertheless, the drive for American independence held a lot of appeal for the Scotch-Irish. In Pennsylvania, where the Scotch-Irish were overwhelmingly on the Patriot side, resentment against the established landowners and governors of the colony was strong. In other locations, grudges against the British had carried over to America from Ulster.

The province of Ulster and the American colonies had common interests in the 18th century. Both were dependencies of the British crown but (unlike Scotland) were not actually part of Great Britain. The residents of Ulster and of the American colonies could not send representatives to the British Parliament and resented Parliament's power to govern them and, particularly, to tax them. The Scotch-Irish in Ulster who were Presbyterians were continually reminded that their church was not the established church. They were even forced to contribute money to the Anglican church—a church that they not only did not belong to but strongly disagreed with. English landlords had imposed impossibly high rents, and the English Parliament had made laws that inhibited the ability of

John Paul Jones led in the capture of the British warship Serapis *off Britain's North Sea coast. Early in the battle, the captain of the* Serapis *asked Jones if he was ready to surrender yet. Jones replied defiantly, "I have not yet begun to fight."*

the Scotch-Irish to sell their products outside Ireland. They did not want to have their economic and religious liberty tampered with once they were in America. For these reasons they furnished a lot of manpower to the Continental Army to see that this did not happen.

Thomas Polk (who was a great uncle of President James Knox Polk) read a "Mecklenburg Declaration" in North Carolina in 1775 and expressed the sentiments of the Scotch-Irish settlers in America towards British policy: "Resolved, that whosoever...countenanced the unchartered and dangerous invasion of our rights, as claimed by Great Britain, is an enemy to this country—to America—and to the inherent and inalienable rights of man."

The Revolution, however, was no war of words. Many Scots and Scotch-Irish settlers, whether they were Tories or Patriots, paid dearly for their stands. For example, Cherry Valley, a Scotch-Irish settlement of some 60 families in New York's Otsego County, suffered a devastating attack. The Tories of New York's Mohawk Valley and their Native American allies marched into Cherry Valley on October 11, 1778. In the fighting that ensued, 16 soldiers of the rebel Continental Army were killed. Then, to punish the settlers for harboring rebel soldiers, the attackers massacred 32 of the inhabitants, mostly women and children, and took the rest of the residents prisoner. The buildings of Cherry Valley were then burned, and not until about 1785 did any of the survivors return to rebuild the settlement.

Military Leaders

No strangers to military operations, the Scots and Scotch-Irish provided the Patriot cause with some of its most illustrious military leaders during the Revolution.

John Paul Jones was the leading naval hero of the Revolutionary War. He had been born in the parish of Kirkbeam in Kirkcudbrightshire, Scotland, and came to America at the beginning of the Revolution. The Continental Congress entrusted him with the command of several small ships. He cruised for some time off the coast of his native Scotland and captured some British merchant vessels. In 1779, he was given command of a French ship that he renamed the *Bonhomme Richard* (*Poor Richard*) after Benjamin Franklin's famous almanac. In September 1779, his vessel won in an engagement with the *Serapis*, a much larger English warship. Captain Pearson, commander of the *Serapis,* asked Jones if he was ready to give up, since the fight seemed to be going badly at that point for the *Bonhomme Richard*. Jones gave the now-famous reply, "I have not yet begun to fight."

John Stark, of Scotch-Irish descent, was born at Londonderry, New Hampshire, in 1728. He knew the frontier country well and served with distinction in the French and Indian War. At the outbreak of the Revolutionary War, he received a colonel's commission and fought the British at Bunker Hill. He resigned from the army soon after this and formed an independent corps. When the British General John Burgoyne sent a force into New Hampshire to collect supplies, Stark's troops went after them. In August 1777, when American and British forces clashed near Bennington, Vermont, Stark's army scored a big victory. Burgoyne had to continue south without supplies, and his army was soon defeated and captured at the Battle of Saratoga, the decisive battle that convinced the French to ally themselves with the Americans. Congress appointed Stark a brigadier general, and he served throughout the war.

Henry Knox, who was born in Boston on July 25, 1750, of County Antrim stock, fought the British at the Battle of Bunker Hill. He was commissioned

a colonel of the artillery and served throughout the Revolutionary War, being advanced to major general in 1782. Knox later became secretary of war in George Washington's first cabinet.

Colonel George Rogers Clark, a Scotch-Irish adventurer, was commissioned in 1780 by Governor Patrick Henry of Virginia to organize and lead an expedition against certain British forts in the interior. Clark led the expedition overland in the winter months, enduring great physical hardships. The British were completely surprised, however, by this offseason assault. Clark's victories, especially at Vincennes in what is now Indiana, established such a strong claim on the Northwest Territory that the British ceded the territory to the United States at the end of the Revolutionary War. Clark's younger brother William accompanied Meriwether Lewis on the famous Lewis and Clark expedition to the Northwest in 1806.

General Anthony Wayne (whose willingness to lead daring charges earned him the nickname "Mad Anthony") was born of Ulster parents in Pennsylvania. His greatest achievement was the storming and capture of Stony Point on the Hudson River in New York. Colonel William Campbell, whose family had immigrated to America from Ulster, led American troops in a decisive victory over the British at King's Mountain, North Carolina, on October 7, 1780. In another American victory—at the Battle of Cowpers, South Carolina, on January 17, 1781—two Scotch-Irish Americans distinguished themselves. One hero of this battle was Daniel Morgan, an elder of the Presbyterian Church, who was born in Ballinascreen, in County Londonderry, Northern Ireland. Also, the

James Wilson of Pennsylvania

leader of the American forces was Major Joseph McDowell, whose father had emigrated from Ulster.

Among the most famous segments of the Continental Army was called the Pennsylvania Line. Seven companies of this regiment were composed almost exclusively of Scotch-Irish soldiers. Contemporary witnesses reported that these frontier troops were excellent shots and frequently able to hit targets far beyond normal shooting range.

Laying the Foundation

Outside the military arena, Americans of Scots and Scotch-Irish descent were making major contributions to the cause of independence. Seven of the 56 signers of the Declaration of Independence were Scots or Scotch-Irish. Two, Thomas McKean and John Hancock, were American-born. James Wilson and John Witherspoon had been born in Scotland. Three (James Smith, Matthew Thornton, and George Taylor) had been born in Ulster.

Patrick Henry, the first governor of the new Commonwealth of Virginia, was a Scot and a fiery patriot famous for his slogan, "Give me liberty or give me death." He was born in Hanover County, Virginia, but his father had immigrated to America from Aberdeen, Scotland. No colonial leader was more outspoken on behalf of independence from Great Britain.

Nine of the first governors of the 13 newly created states were Scots or Scotch-Irish: George Clinton of New York, Thomas McKean of Pennsylvania, William Livingston of New Jersey, Patrick Henry of Virginia, John MacKinley of Delaware, Richard Caswell of North Carolina, John Rutledge of South Carolina, Archibald Bulloch of Georgia, and Jonathan Trumbull of Connecticut. George Clinton of New York served in the

Revolutionary War and was seven times elected governor of that state. He was also twice elected vice president of the United States (under Presidents Thomas Jefferson and James Madison).

George Washington's cabinet included Alexander Hamilton, who was part Scottish, as secretary of the treasury. Washington also appointed Henry Knox as secretary of war and Edmund Randolph as attorney general. The first Supreme Court included James Wilson and John Blair, both of whom were Scots, and John Rutledge, an Ulster Scot.

George Clinton

John C. Calhoun served in a variety of posts during the early days of the American republic. He served as secretary of war under President Monroe and as a senator from South Carolina, and he was elected vice president in 1824 and 1828. His disagreement with Andrew Jackson over the issue of states' rights probably cost him a chance at the office of president.

A Role in the Nation's Growth

The American colonies had won their independence, but they faced a great deal of hard work in refining the government of the new nation and developing its economy. As they had in the founding of the United States, the Scots and Scotch-Irish played a significant part in helping the United States grow.

The War of 1812

The War of 1812 went favorably for the United States partly because of the actions of two American naval officers of Scottish descent. Oliver Hazard Perry, born in Rhode Island, became one of the heroes of that war. Captain Perry was given the job of equipping a squadron and keeping the British from controlling Lake Erie. His fleet defeated the British squadron at

Captain Oliver Hazard Perry's flagship was disabled in a battle with the British ship Niagara. Perry, however, was rowed to the Niagara and his forces eventually captured it. Perry's victory secured American control of Lake Erie during the War of 1812.

Put-in-Bay, off Ohio's Bass Islands, in September 1813. This was a significant victory for the Americans, who had feared a lake-borne invasion of their country by the British. Perry's short report to his immediate commander, General William Henry Harrison, was, "We have met the enemy and they are ours: two ships, two brigs, one schooner, and one sloop."

Thomas Macdonough, born in Delaware, entered the United States Navy and served in the Tripolitan War off the coast of what is now Libya. He assisted Captain Stephen Decatur in the burning of the *Philadelphia*, a ship that the Tripolitan pirates had captured. During the War of 1812, Macdonough was put in charge of the American squadron on Lake Champlain and had the task of keeping the British from invading the United States by that water route. He defeated an enemy squadron at the Battle of Plattsburg on September 11, 1814. This naval victory, along with Perry's, ensured American control of the inland waterways.

Sir Edward Pakenham, the British commander, landed an army at New Orleans with the intention of capturing the city. General Jackson, fresh from his victory over the Creek tribe of Native Americans at Horseshoe Bend, stationed his Kentucky and Tennessee rifle squadrons behind cotton bales to defend the city. The British soldiers attacked across open ground and were cut down in large numbers. General Pakenham was killed, and the British suffered nearly 2,000 casualties. The Americans lost only 13 men. The British expedition withdrew in defeat, and Andrew Jackson became a hero.

The War for Texan Independence

In the 1830s, when Americans who had settled in the Mexican territory of Texas decided to secede from Mexico and set up their own state, two Americans of Scotch-Irish descent entered the fray.

Samuel Houston, soldier and statesman, was born in Rockbridge County, Virginia. His paternal ancestors were Ulster Scots who had migrated to Pennsylvania and later to Virginia in the first part of the 18th century. He served under Andrew Jackson during the War of 1812 and was wounded at the Battle of Horseshoe Bend on March 28, 1814. Houston led the Texas forces when they defeated the army of General Santa Anna at the Battle of

Thomas Macdonough prevented the British from taking control of Lake Champlain during the War of 1812. This portrait was painted by another Scots-American, Gilbert Stuart.

The War of 1812 ended with the signing of the Treaty of Ghent in December 1814. Unfortunately, communications were so slow that word did not reach the United States for several weeks. As a result, the famous Scotch-Irish frontier fighter and later president, Andrew Jackson, led his men in a battle against the British army at New Orleans in January 1815, even though the war had been over for a month.

38

San Jacinto on April 21, 1836. Texas won its independence as a result of this battle, and Houston became the first president of the Texas Republic on October 22, 1836. He served as a U.S. senator after Texas was annexed to the United States in 1845, and in the 1850s he was elected governor of the state. He lost this position when he opposed secession from the Union.

David Crockett was born in Hawkins County, Tennessee, a heavily Scotch-Irish area. (His father fought in the battle of King's Mountain in the American Revolution.) Davy Crockett became a frontier legend as humorous exaggerations of his skill—at everything from killing bears to jumping fences—entered American folklore. He was, however, also an influential political figure who served several terms representing Kentucky in the U.S. House of Representatives. Crockett later moved to Texas and lost his life helping in the defense of the Alamo in San Antonio in 1836.

Davy Crockett and other defenders of the Alamo were eventually overrun by the forces of Mexico's General Santa Anna.

Another American frontier hero, Christopher (Kit) Carson, was of Scots descent. He was born in Kentucky, but his grandfather, William Carson, was an immigrant from Scotland who had settled in North Carolina. Kit Carson became a trapper, guide, and soldier. He first gained prominence by serving as Lt. John Charles Frémont's guide on western expeditions and later as a soldier during the Mexican War.

The Civil War

Many officers of Scottish descent served with distinction in the American Civil War. Among the many Scots-descended generals on the Union side were Generals Ulysses S. Grant and George Brinton McClellan.

General Ulysses S. Grant was an officer on the western front in the early years of the Civil War. His greatest achievement during that period was the siege and capture of Vicksburg. Lincoln ordered him east to take charge of the Union forces after General George Meade failed to follow up the victory over Confederate troops under General Robert E. Lee at Gettysburg. Grant continued to attack Lee, but only at a terrible loss in Union troops. Lincoln resisted the pressures that were put upon him to remove Grant, saying that he was the first Union general who seemed to keep the Union armies moving after Lee and the Confederates. Grant's tenacity and

General Jeb Stuart of the Confederate Army

aggressiveness paid off, and Lee was forced to retreat towards Richmond in 1865. When Lee's lines were threatened near Richmond, he moved his armies west, hoping to join forces with other Confederate troops. Grant moved ahead of him, however, and Lee was forced to surrender to Grant at Appomattox Court House, Virginia, on April 9, 1865.

General George Brinton McClellan had ancestors who had come from Scotland to the United States early in the 18th century. (His great-grandfather, Samuel McClellan, served in the Revolutionary War.) McClellan entered West Point in 1842 and was in command of the Army of the Potomac at the start of the Civil War. His armies met those of Lee in two important battles, the Peninsular Campaign and Antietam. Lee was said to have remarked once that McClellan was the best Union general he ever faced. McClellan ran for the office of president on the Democratic ticket in 1864 and was defeated by Lincoln.

Many of the officers serving the Confederacy were also of Scottish descent. General Thomas Jonathan Jackson, a West Point graduate, served in the Mexican War and taught at the Virginia Military Institute. His forces participated in the First Battle of Bull Run. "There is Jackson standing like a stone wall," a remark attributed to Brigadier General Barnard E. Bee, began the legend of Stonewall Jackson. General Jackson worked perfectly with Robert E. Lee, and together they inflicted many costly defeats on the Union armies. He was shot by his own men on May 2, 1863, when returning to the lines after a scouting expedition. His loss was a great blow to General Lee and the South.

General James Ewell Brown Stuart was one of the South's finest officers. Known as Jeb, he assisted General

Union General George Brinton McClellan

Lee by undertaking risky scouting expeditions. He was wounded in action on May 11, 1864, and he died the following day.

19th-Century Immigration

Many of the Scots who left the United States during and after the Revolution went to Spanish Florida, Canada, and England. Bad harvests in 1782 and 1783 caused a new burst of emigration from Scotland, but as a result of the Revolution, the stream of immigrants shifted from North Carolina and New York to Canada—especially to Ontario, Nova Scotia, and Prince Edward Island. The same was true when a major famine struck Scotland in the 1840s. Most of the emigrants went to Canada.

Later in the 19th century, the United States again attracted significant numbers of Scottish immigrants, mostly industrial workers. The industrial base in the United States was larger than Canada's, so it offered more hope of a job. Throughout the late 19th and early 20th centuries, immigration from Scotland remained strong. When unemployment reached particularly bad levels in Scotland, the number of Scots newly arrived in the United States would rise. The period of greatest Scottish immigration to America was the decade of the 1920s, when the Scottish economy was in a deep depression. More than 300,000 Scots came to the United States in those 10 years, an average of more than 30,000 a year.

At the beginning of the 19th century, the Scots stayed away from America because they wanted to, but many Scotch-Irish stayed away because they had to. Various British laws made it illegal for skilled workers to leave British territory, and after 1783 the United States was no longer British territory. Numerous Scotch-Irish workers managed to find their way to the United States anyway—sometimes by going to Canada first and then to the U.S.—but the restrictions almost certainly kept the number of immigrants down. After the end of the War of 1812, when such laws were no longer enforced, immigration picked up substantially.

In the pre-Revolutionary period, immigrants from Scotland and Ulster had come in only modest numbers, but they often rose to prominence soon after arriving in America. In the 19th century, although Scottish and Scotch-Irish immigrants came in larger numbers, they did not make such an immediate impact. One of the reasons was the sheer volume of immigrants from many other nations—more than one million a year at some points during the 19th century. In such a crush of immigrants, it was harder for the Scots and Scotch-Irish to stand out.

Nevertheless, some of the most illustrious names in U.S. history are those of the Scots and Scotch-Irish in America.

General Ulysses S. Grant (wearing wide-brimmed hat) and his staff gathered outside their command tent. This photo was taken by the famed Civil War photographer Mathew B. Brady.

4
CONTRIBUTIONS TO AMERICAN LIFE

Juanita M. Kreps

Government and Public Affairs

Scottish and Scotch-Irish political power in the United States has been substantial since the founding of the nation. Eleven U.S. presidents have been of Scottish or Scotch-Irish descent: James Monroe (president from 1817 to 1825), Andrew Jackson (1829-1837), James K. Polk (1845-1849), James Buchanan (1857-1861), Andrew Johnson (1865-1869), Ulysses S. Grant (1869-1877), Chester A. Arthur (1881-1885), William McKinley (1897-1901), Woodrow Wilson (1913-1921), and Lyndon B. Johnson (1963-1969).

The number of Scots and Scotch-Irish members of presidential cabinets is huge. One outstanding example is Juanita M. Kreps, who was secretary of commerce from 1977 to 1979. Born Juanita Morris in Lynch, Kentucky, in 1921, she became a noted professor of economics at Duke University in North Carolina. In 1972, she rose to national prominence as the first woman to be director of the New York Stock Exchange. When President Jimmy Carter appointed her to his cabinet in 1977, she scored another first—no other woman had ever been secretary of commerce.

When the United Nations was being established in 1945, one of the U.S. representatives to the conference of founders was Adlai E. Stevenson. Stevenson, from Illinois, belonged to a Scots family that had long been politically prominent. (His grandfather had served as vice president under President Grover Cleveland.) Twice nominated by the Democratic Party for president of the United States, Stevenson lost both times to President Dwight D. Eisenhower. More work on the international level, however, lay ahead for Stevenson, who was appointed U.S. ambassador to the United Nations during the Kennedy administration. He held that post until his death in 1965.

Another Democratic nominee for president of the United States, George McGovern of South Dakota, is of Scots descent. While representing South Dakota in the U.S. Senate, McGovern voiced strong criticism of U.S. involvement in Vietnam. Seen as an advocate of liberal social policies and of reform within his own party, he captured the Democratic nomination to run against the Republican incumbent, Richard M. Nixon, for president in 1972. In that historic election campaign, Republican

George McGovern

tactics included the notorious break-in at Democratic Party offices in the Watergate office building. McGovern lost to Nixon, but revelations about Republican election activities eventually put several of Nixon's closest aides in prison and forced the president to resign. McGovern continued to represent South Dakota in the Senate throughout the 1970s and launched another unsuccessful try for the presidency in 1984.

General Douglas MacArthur wades ashore at the Philippine island of Leyte in 1944.
When his troops were forced to evacuate their positions at Bataan and Corregidor in
1942, MacArthur had promised to return to the Philippines.

General Douglas MacArthur, one of the eminent military leaders of World War II and the postwar period, was very proud of his Scottish ancestors. His grandfather came to America in 1825 and later became governor of Wisconsin and a federal judge. His father was General Arthur MacArthur, who served in the Union Army during the Civil War, was a colonel at the age of 20, and later became the military governor of the Philippine Islands.

Douglas MacArthur grew up on Army frontier posts. He went to West Point and graduated first in his class in 1903. During World War I, he became a brigadier general and was wounded in action. When the Japanese attacked Pearl Harbor in December 1941, MacArthur was in the Philippines helping to arrange for Philippine independence from the United States. Japan's rapid invasion of Southeast Asia in late 1941 and early 1942, however, put independence on hold. The Japanese swept through the Philippines, and MacArthur's troops were beseiged on the Bataan Peninsula and on Corregidor Island in Manila Bay, where they held out until March 1942. President Franklin D. Roosevelt eventually ordered MacArthur to evacuate his positions, but MacArthur vowed he would return to the Philippines, which he did in a dramatic landing on the island of Leyte in 1944.

Perhaps his greatest accomplishment, however, was MacArthur's humane and farsighted treatment of the Japanese after World War II. As the chief American official in occupied Japan, MacArthur refused to adopt harsh or vengeful policies against the defeated Japanese. Later, MacArthur commanded the troops of the United Nations in the Korean War, but he and President Harry Truman had a falling out over whether U.N. forces should invade China. Truman stripped MacArthur of his command in 1951, after which MacArthur essentially retired to write his memoirs. He died in 1964.

The momentous first step from Apollo 11's landing module onto the moon's surface was taken by an American of Scots descent. Neil Alden Armstrong, born in Ohio in 1930, was a veteran astronaut when he joined the Apollo

Astronaut Neil A. Armstrong during a practice for Apollo 11's mission to the moon

11 expedition to the moon. On July 20, 1969, Armstrong descended the landing module's ladder and went for a brief walk—the first time a human being strolled a landscape beyond earth.

One of the foremost labor leaders in U.S. history, Philip Murray, was born in Blantyre, Scotland, in 1886. After moving to the United States in 1902, he worked as a miner and eventually rose to the vice presidency of the United Mine Workers of America. This

John Muir was a major force in the establishment of the U.S. system of national parks and national forests. He also founded the Sierra Club, an influential private group dedicated to the protection of America's natural environment.

labor union was the largest member of the Congress of Industrial Organizations (CIO), a confederation of unions. In the early 1940s, Murray took over the presidency of the CIO from John L. Lewis. Under Murray, the CIO cooperated with U.S. government industrial policies during World War II and, after the war, expelled several unions that the CIO leadership considered Communist-controlled.

Douglas Fraser, another U.S. labor leader born in Scotland, was a leading figure among unionized automobile workers. Born in Glasgow in 1916, Fraser came to the U.S. as a child in 1922 and settled in Detroit, the hub of the U.S. automobile industry. While working for the Chrysler Corporation, he was active in union affairs and served as a vice president of the United Automobile Workers Union from 1977 to 1983.

The conservationist John Muir, even though he was never elected to any public office, had a profound effect on U.S. land-use policy. Muir was born at Dunbar, Scotland, in 1838 and immigrated to the United States in 1849 when his family took up farming near Portage, Wisconsin. His overriding interest in life was the appreciation and preservation of America's forests and other wild country. When Sequoia and Yosemite national parks were established in 1890, Muir deserved a large measure of the credit. His efforts to set aside numerous tracts of uncut forest, however, met with much greater opposition from logging interests. Muir persisted—writing persuasive magazine articles and even taking President Theodore Roosevelt on a camping trip in 1903—and the National Forest system was eventually created. Muir also founded the Sierra Club, a conservationist organization, in 1892. In 1908, two wooded regions north of San Francisco were set aside for conservation and were named Muir Woods National Monument in his honor. John Muir died soon afterward, just before Christmas in 1914.

Labor leader Philip Murray

Business and Industry

Andrew Carnegie, one of the wealthiest industrialists in U.S. history, was born at Dunfermlime, Scotland, in 1835. The son of a handloom weaver, he came with his family to America in 1848 and settled at Allegheny, Pennsylvania. Carnegie became the personal secretary and private telegrapher for Thomas Scott of the Pennsylvania Railroad, and so began the career that led him to build a huge industrial empire. Eventually he owned his own iron ore mines, coal mines, steamship lines, railroad lines, and steel mills. In 1900, the profits of Carnegie's businesses totaled about $40 million, a massive amount of money at that time. Carnegie donated much of his wealth—about $350 million by 1919—to such projects as the building of libraries and the endowment of universities. He died in 1919 and was buried at Sleepy Hollow on the Hudson River.

Born in Ulster in 1803, James Gamble came with his family to the United States in 1819 and settled in Cincinnati. He entered the soapmaking business and, in 1837, went into partnership with his brother-in-law, William Procter. Procter was a candlemaker who used many of the same basic materials in candlemaking as Gamble used in soapmaking. An attention to basic ingredients paid off for the firm of Procter & Gamble, especially when, by anticipating that the American Civil War would interrupt supplies of crucial

Ivory soap was first marketed by Procter & Gamble in the 1870s.

James Gamble

James N. Gamble

materials, they stockpiled these materials before the war. Famous for their *Ivory* soap and for countless other familiar products—*Tide* laundry detergent, *Crest* toothpaste, and *Crisco* shortening, for example—Procter & Gamble diversified greatly, especially after control passed to Harley Procter and James N. Gamble, the sons of the founders.

The Mellon family from Ulster became one of richest and most influential families in the United States. Thomas Mellon was born in Northern Ireland in 1813 and immigrated to the U.S. as a child. One of Pittsburgh's most successful bankers, he provided the ideal business for his son, Andrew W. Mellon, to enter. Andrew Mellon proved to be an exceptionally shrewd banker and later served as secretary of the treasury under Presidents Harding, Coolidge, and Hoover and as the U.S. ambassador to Great Britain from 1932 through 1933. Mellon also donated millions of dollars worth of money and art to establish the National Gallery of Art in Washington, D.C.

Numerous other Americans of Scots or Scotch-Irish descent were prominent in business during the 19th and early 20th centuries. Marcus Alonzo Hanna, a wealthy Cleveland industrialist and politician, had Scotch-Irish ancestors. Philip Danforth Armour, another Scotch-Irishman, made a fortune

Andrew Carnegie

as a meat packer and grain dealer in Chicago and was one of the first in his industry to take advantage of refrigerated railroad cars to transport meat.

Leon Leonwood Bean ran a small men's-clothing store in Maine for many years before he began selling a new product that was to turn his business around. In 1912, he developed what he called the Maine Hunting Shoe, a boot with an upper section made of leather and a waterproof lower section coated with rubber. Sold by mail, this boot was so successful that Bean

51

James S. McDonnell

1967, the company continued to be run by members of his family.

J. Willard Marriott, who established the well-known chain of hotels named after him, was born in Utah in 1900. He got his start in business by operating a root beer stand in Washington, D.C., a business that he later expanded into a full restaurant, the Hot Shoppe. His business continued to prosper after he won a contract to supply Eastern Airlines with catered meals to serve on their flights. In 1957, he started his hotel operations by opening the Twin Bridges Marriott Motor Hotel in Washington, D.C. By the time of Marriott's death in 1985, the company had become one of the largest chains of hotels in the world with operations in 26 countries.

One of the most energetic and influential aerospace pioneers in U.S. history, James S. McDonnell, liked to joke that his outstanding achievements were simply ordinary for the Scots. Born in Denver in 1899, he was trained as an engineer and in 1939 became president of McDonnell Aircraft, a company that supplied jet airplanes for U.S. aircraft carriers during World War II. Later, McDonnell Aircraft produced space capsules and rocket components for the U.S. space program. In 1967,

began to sell other men's clothing, mostly items related to outdoor activities, by mail. His catalogs became popular for their writing as well as for the products they advertised, and they helped turn the L. L. Bean company of Freeport, Maine, into one of the most successful mail-order clothing firms in the U.S. Even after Bean died in

J. Willard Marriott in the doorway of his restaurant in Washington, D.C.

McDonnell Aircraft merged with another company founded by a Scots-descended giant of American aviation—the Douglas Corporation, established in 1920 by Donald Douglas (1892-1981). Douglas retired after the merger, and McDonnell became chairman and chief executive officer of McDonnell Douglas Corporation, a major manufacturer of aerospace equipment. He served as chairman of McDonnell Douglas until his death in 1980.

In 1892, Alexander Graham Bell made the first telephone call between New York and Chicago.

Inventors

As the United States grew to be an industrial and agricultural power during the 19th century, numerous Americans of Scots and Scotch-Irish descent contributed invaluable inventions.

Robert Fulton did not invent the steam engine or even the steamboat, but his design for the *Clermont*—which was launched in 1807 on the Hudson River in New York—showed that steamships could be operated at a profit. (His partner in the *Clermont* project, the diplomat Robert Livingston, was also of Scots descent.) A versatile person with wide-ranging interests, Fulton also was an accomplished artist, devised new ways of operating canals, invented a ropemaking machine, and experimented with designs for submarines and underwater guns.

The invention of the reaper, a machine that revolutionized American agriculture, was the work of Cyrus McCormick, an American of Scotch-Irish descent. Born in Virginia in 1809, McCormick had the good fortune of introducing his mechanical reaping machine at a time when American agriculture had spread to the prairies of the Midwest. On large farms and relatively flat ground, such as the prairie, a machine that could be towed over the farm to cut a crop was extremely practical. McCormick was also a competent businessman and established an effective production and distribution network for his machines.

Alexander Graham Bell, the inventor of the telephone and an outstanding figure in the education of the deaf, was born in Edinburgh in 1847, immigrated to Canada at the age of 23, and moved to the United States in 1872. The dramatic, well-known scene in which Bell summons his assistant, Thomas A. Watson, from another room with the first understandable sentences transmitted by telephone— "Mr. Watson, come here. I want you"— occurred in 1876. By the summer of 1877, the Bell Telephone Company had been established and it was possible— for the very few people who had telephones—to converse between Boston and New York. The Bell Telephone Company spawned some of the world's largest companies—such as American Telephone & Telegraph, International Telephone & Telegraph, and Bell Laboratories. Bell never lost his love for his native Scotland. He purchased a large estate in Nova Scotia where he spent his summers in surroundings that reminded him of the Scottish countryside. He died in 1922, and all telephone service throughout the

Cyrus McCormick's reaper was first publicly tested in 1831.

Nassau Hall at Princeton University, now a National Historic Landmark, was opened in 1756. All of Princeton's classrooms and dormitories were in this one building until the early 1800s.

North American continent was suspended for one full minute during his burial service.

Education and Scholarship

The Scotch-Irish Presbyterians were the first religious group to found institutions of higher learning in Pennsylvania. Since they were particularly numerous in the Cumberland Valley, they established Dickinson College at Carlisle, which was the first denominational school in Pennsylvania and the 12th college to be founded in the United States. Washington and Jefferson College in western Pennsylvania was also a Scotch-Irish institution. Other institutions in which Scotch-Irish Presbyterians have been influential are Allegheny College, Waynesburg College, Westminster College, and Geneva College, all in Pennsylvania.

The Scotch-Irish also had a part in the establishment of Transylvania College and Centre College in Kentucky and Wooster College in Ohio.

In 1746, the College of New Jersey, only the fourth institute of higher learning to be established in what is now the United States, was founded at Elizabeth, New Jersey. Originally founded by Presbyterians, the college changed locations twice, finally settling in Princeton, in central New Jersey. Eventually, at the end of the 19th century, the college adopted the name of this city and became Princeton University.

The college's most vigorous period of growth began when Dr. John Witherspoon came over from Scotland in 1768 to take charge. It graduated only 230 students from 1766 to 1773, but from this group emerged 12 members of the Continental Congress, 24 members of the Congress of the United States, three justices of the Supreme Court, five cabinet members, one president, and one vice president.

Princeton University has long enjoyed a solid reputation as one of the best universities in the United States. On Princeton's roll of distinguished faculty members through nearly 250 years of history is a German refugee named Dr. Albert Einstein.

Hampden-Sydney College in Virginia was founded in 1774, with the active support and approval of the Hanover Presbytery. Its location in Prince Edward County was chosen so that it would be convenient for the Scotch-Irish settlements in Virginia and North Carolina. The first president of the college, the Reverend Stanhope Smith, was a graduate of the College of New Jersey.

William Holmes McGuffey, an educator and the compiler of a series of reading texts for schools, was born in Washington County, Pennsylvania, and settled near Youngstown, Ohio, in 1802. He graduated from Washington College in 1826 and became a professor and then president of several colleges and universities. His fame, however, rests on his *Eclectic Readers* for elementary schools. While he was a professor at Miami University in Ohio, he began a series of schoolbooks. The six-book series he eventually produced went through many editions, and a huge number of them—122 million copies—were sold.

A Scots-descended professor of economics at Harvard University, John Kenneth Galbraith, was born in 1908 at Iona Station, Ontario. After moving from Canada to the United States to earn a doctoral degree in agricultural economics, Galbraith became an influential voice in U.S. politics. Besides his well-known books about economics—such as *The Affluent Society*—Galbraith wrote speeches for Democratic politicians such as John F. Kennedy, Eugene McCarthy, and George McGovern. Among economists, he is known for his theories about the distribution of economic

Henry James

known ancestor was Sir Richard de Melvill, who was forced, in 1296, to swear allegiance to King Edward I of England when Edward conquered Scotland.) Melville went to sea at 18, and his books frequently tell of sea voyages and adventuring in remote places. His other works include the novels *Omoo*, *Typee*, *White Jacket*, and *Billy Budd*.

Washington Irving (1783-1859), the son of a deacon who was a Scottish Covenanter (someone who has pledged to defend Presbyterianism), is best

power among producers, consumers, and the government.

Another prominent American scholar is Gilbert Highet. Born in Glasgow, Dr. Highet eventually became chair of the department of Greek and Latin at Columbia University in New York City.

Literature and the Arts

Herman Melville (1819-1891), the author of one of America's literary classics, *Moby Dick*, was born in New York, but he is descended from a long line of prominent Scots. (His earliest

Herman Melville

known as the author of "The Legend of Sleepy Hollow," the story of Ichabod Crane's misfortunes one Halloween. Born in New York City, Irving specialized in tales about the Dutch of the Hudson Valley counties just upriver from the city. Another of his popular tales is the story of Rip Van Winkle.

Edgar Allan Poe (1809-1849), the poet and short-story writer, was Scotch-Irish on his father's side. A tumultuous life and a mysterious death have made Poe himself almost as intriguing as his detective stories and his famous tales of the bizarre, such as "The Masque of the Red Death," "The Fall of the House of Usher," and "The Tell-Tale Heart." Just before he was to be married for a second time (his first wife died young), Poe was found unconscious on a Baltimore street and died soon afterwards. No cause of Edgar Allan Poe's death has ever been definitely established.

One Scotch-Irish family produced two of the foremost intellectuals of the late 19th century. William James (1842-1910), philosopher, psychologist, and lecturer, was the author of *The Varieties of Religious Experience*. His brother, Henry James (1843-1916), was a novelist known for such works as *The Turn of the Screw*, *The Ambassadors*, and *Daisy Miller*. Both Henry and William James were born in the United States, but Henry moved to England later in his life and became a naturalized British subject in 1915, a year before his death.

Scots and Scotch-Irish Americans have also made an impact in the visual arts. Gilbert Stuart, a great early American artist, was the son of an immigrant from Perth, Scotland. Stuart's work includes portraits of Presidents Washington, John Adams, Jefferson, Madison, Monroe, and John Quincy Adams, and Kings George III and IV of England and Louis XVII of France. He was considered the foremost portrait painter of his time. George Inness became one of the leading landscape painters in America, and Thomas Eakins, whose paternal grandfather had come to America from Northern

George Inness, an artist who specialized in landscape paintings. Especially during the early part of his career, his work had a pleasant simplicity and brightness.

Ireland, was also an outstanding painter and art teacher. The abstract expressionist painter Robert Burns Motherwell, who was born in Aberdeen, Washington, in 1915, is of Scots descent.

Journalism

The first newspaper printed in America, the *Boston News Letter*, was the work of a Scot named John Campbell. Many other prominent journalists in America have been of Scots or Scotch-Irish ancestry. James Gordon Bennett of the *New York Herald* was responsible for sending Henry M. Stanley to Africa in 1870 to search for Dr. David Livingstone. Horace Greeley went into journalism at an early age and made the *New York Tribune* one of the leading papers of the middle of the 19th century. Greeley also became involved in such reform movements as the drive to abolish slavery. He ran for president on the Democratic ticket in 1872 but was defeated and died soon afterwards. Whitelaw Reid served on the staff of the *Tribune* under Greeley, and upon the latter's death became editor-in-chief. After a successful career in journalism, he became a diplomat and served as minister to France and ambassador to Great Britain. Henry Woodfin Grady, a vigorous advocate of the so-called "New South" after the Civil War, was also a journalist of Scotch-Irish ancestry.

Colonel Robert R. McCormick, publisher of the *Chicago Tribune*, was also of Scottish ancestry. His father had been ambassador to Austria-Hungary, Russia, and France, and the son grew up around the world. He studied law, but he later turned to journalism and was probably the most controversial publisher of the first half of the 20th century. When McCormick died on April 1, 1955, tributes came from such notables as General Douglas MacArthur, a fellow Scot. President Eisenhower spoke of the deaths of McCormick and Joseph Pulitzer, who had died the day before, and said that in their passing "American journalism had lost the services of two of its outstanding publishers."

Malcolm S. Forbes, the adventurous and flashy publisher of *Forbes* magazine from the mid-1960s until 1990, was the son of a Scottish immigrant who founded the magazine in 1917. Forbes attended Princeton and in 1946 joined the staff of the family

Malcolm S. Forbes

magazine as an associate editor. After taking control at *Forbes*, he sought new challenges in such pursuits as yachting and racing. In 1973, he became the first person to fly coast to coast across the United States in a single hot-air balloon. In 1989, just a few months before his death in February 1990, he threw an elaborate 70th birthday party for himself at his villa in the Moroccan port of Tangier. News photos of the party showed Forbes dressed in formal Scottish fashion—coat, tie, and kilt.

Music

Stephen Collins Foster (1826-1864), whose family settled near Lancaster, Pennsylvania, was descended on both sides from Scotch-Irish immigrants. Foster gained a permanent place in American music by composing songs that appealed to a wide audience. Many Foster compositions—such as "The Old Folks at Home," "O Susanna," "My Old Kentucky Home," and "Jeanie with the Light Brown Hair"—have become such standards that many Americans know them without even considering who wrote them. Foster spent his last years in poverty and obscurity and died in 1860, after a short illness in the charity ward of the Bellevue Hospital in New York City.

Edward Alexander MacDowell (1860-1908), another distinguished musician of Scottish ancestry, was born in New York City. He composed classical works, mostly for symphony orchestra and for piano, and spent much of his time touring Europe and America. Some of his compositions are *Woodland Sketches*, *Indian Suite*, and *Sea Pieces*.

Scotland has been fertile territory for rock musicians and can claim such accomplished performers as Mark Knopfler (of Dire Straits and the Notting Hillbillies), David Knopfler, and

Stephen Collins Foster

Annie Lennox (of Eurythmics). Sheena Easton, although she spends much of her time performing in the United States, remains a British subject and has not officially immigrated to America.

One major figure in modern music who has immigrated from Scotland to the United States is David Byrne, perhaps best known as the lead singer for Talking Heads. Byrne was born at Dumbarton, Scotland, in 1952 and came with his family to the United States six years later. Talking Heads, although long considered part of pop music's arty fringe, had a major hit in "Burning Down the House" from the 1983 album *Speaking in Tongues*. Byrne's own accomplishments, however, range much further than rock music. He co-wrote and directed the 1986 film *True Stories*, and he received an Academy Award in 1987 for his part in composing the orchestral score for the film *The Last Emperor*. Byrne also developed a strong interest in the popular music of Brazil and released a multivolume compilation of classic Brazilian songs.

David Byrne

Sports

In the early days of American football, John Bain ("Jock") Sutherland was an accomplished defensive player and an influential coach. Sutherland was born in 1889 in Coupar-Angus,

Robert Yale Lary

Scotland, and immigrated to the United States at the age of 18. He played his college football at the University of Pittsburgh, where his coach was the legendary Pop Warner. Sutherland later became a coach himself for the University of Pittsburgh, the Brooklyn Dodgers, and finally the Pittsburgh Steelers. He died in 1948.

Robert Yale Lary, who was born in 1930 at Fort Worth, Texas, is of Scotch-Irish ancestry. Best known as Yale Lary, he claims some of football's best punting statistics—including a career average of 44.28 yards per punt—but also made his mark as a punt returner and as a defensive back. He had more than 50 pass interceptions to his credit in an 11-year career. Lary signed with the Detroit Lions in 1951 and played for the team for two years before being called away for two years of military service. Back with the Lions in 1956, he continued to play for them until his retirement in 1965. During that time, however, he also served in the Texas state legislature for four years. Yale Lary was inducted into the Pro Football Hall of Fame in 1979.

Cyclist Greg LeMond may have a French name, but his family traces its roots to Scotland. (The French name came from a Huguenot ancestor who immigrated to Scotland long ago.) Born in 1961 in California, LeMond became the first American cyclist to win the World Professional Championship (in 1983). Even that achievement was topped, however, in 1986—when LeMond became the first non-European to win the most prestigious cycling race of them all, the Tour de France. After suffering serious gunshot wounds in a hunting accident in 1987, LeMond was nearly forced to give up cycling, but he recovered and went on to take the Tour de France again in 1989 with an 8-second margin of victory. In 1990, he made it two in a row. In the final stages of the 1990 race, LeMond again came from behind to win.

Greg LeMond

Entertainment

Yogi Bear, Fred Flintstone, the Jetsons, and the Smurfs all owe their cartoon lives to an American of Scots descent. William Denby Hanna was born in 1910 in Melrose, New Mexico. In 1937, he went to work for MGM Studios in their cartooning department. There he met his future partner, Joe Barbera, and the two worked together for MGM on the "Tom & Jerry" cartoons. When MGM closed its cartoon studio in 1957, Hanna and Barbera went into business for themselves and first experimented with what would become their specialty—half-hour cartoon shows for television—by airing "Ruff and Reddy" in 1957 and "Huckleberry Hound" in 1958. Many hits

Don Ameche (left) starred with Hume Cronyn (center) and Wilford Brimley in Cocoon *and* Cocoon: The Return. *(This scene is from the latter.) Ameche is of mixed Scotch-Irish, Italian, and German descent.*

John Wayne played the title role in Cahill, United States Marshal.

followed, and Hanna-Barbera Productions eventually branched out into other projects, including live-action dramas like *The Gathering*, a 1977 Christmas story starring Ed Asner.

A film actor who became almost as much a symbol as an actor is also of Scotch-Irish ancestry. John Wayne was born in 1907 in Iowa and was originally christened Marion Michael Morrison. In his first acting job, he worked under the name Duke Morrison, but he later adopted the name under which he is best known. His first lead part was in the 1939 John Ford film *Stagecoach*, and he made

The late Elvis Presley has become an American cultural institution. His ancestry can be traced to one Andrew Presley, Jr., who came to America from Scotland in 1745.

many other films under Ford's direction throughout his career. Some of his best-known films include 1949's *The Sands of Iwo Jima* (for which he received an Academy Award nomination as best actor), *The Man Who Shot Liberty Valance* (1962), and the only film for which he ever won an Oscar, *True Grit* (1969). He also directed *The Alamo* (1960) and *The Green Berets* (1968). Near the end of his career, he became a vocal supporter of conservative political positions and often spoke out about the need for patriotism in America.

The Scots and Scotch-Irish have assimilated so well into the general population of the United States that they do not often stand out as an obvious ethnic group. Since the earliest days of British settlement in North America, they have farmed American land, built American cities, and helped govern American society. Still, their contributions—from the telephone to John Wayne westerns—are daily reminders of the ingenuity of the Scots and Scotch-Irish in America.

INDEX

ACKNOWLEDGMENTS The photographs in this book are reproduced through the courtesy of: p. 2, Thomas J. Lipton Co.; p. 6, Alexandria (Virginia) Convention Visitors Bureau; p. 9, Department of History, Presbyterian Church (U.S.A.); p. 12, Central Office of Information, London; p. 14, Christabel D. Grant; pp. 16, 17, 21, 22, 25, 26, 29, 30, 32, 54, 55, 58 (top and bottom), Independent Picture Service; pp. 18, 20, Frontier Culture Musueum of Virginia; p. 27, North Carolina Travel and Tourism Division; pp. 34, 35, 36, 37, 51, 59, 60, 62, 71 (right), Library of Congress; p. 38, National Gallery of Art, Washington, D.C.; p. 39, Friends of the Governor's Mansion, Austin, Texas; pp. 40, 41, 43, U.S. Signal Corps, National Archives; p. 44, U.S. Department of Commerce; p. 45, George McGovern; p. 46, National Archives; p. 47, NASA; p. 48, State Historical Society of Wisconsin; p. 49, United Steelworkers of America; p. 50 (all), Procter & Gamble; p. 52, McDonnell Douglas; pp. 53, 71 (left), Marriott Corporation; p. 56, Princeton University; p. 61, Harry Benson for Forbes Publishing Co.; p. 63, Nancy Ellison; pp. 66, 68, Hollywood Book and Poster; p. 64, Detroit Lions; pp. 65, 72, Coors Brewing Company; p. 67, Warner Bros., Inc.

J. Willard Marriott   *Lyndon Baines Johnson*

THE *IN AMERICA* SERIES

Lerner Publications Company
241 First Avenue North · Minneapolis, Minnesota 55401